Mommy's Cooking Healthy

Mommy's Cooking Healthy
Southern Style

Introducing 28 Simple Vegetarian and Vegan Meals for Your Family

Alicia Alexandria *Johnson*

Mill City Press, Inc.
2301 Lucien Way #415
Maitland, FL 32751
407.339.4217
www.millcitypress.net

Printed in the United States of America

ISBN-13: 9781545647059

Table Contents:

Introduction 1

Seven Breakfast Meals. 5

Seven Lunch Meals 23

Seven Dinner Meals. 41

Bonus Features: Seven Snacks 61

Hydration Station. 77

Words of Encouragement 79

Testimonial Reviews. 87

Acknowledgements 93

Index 97

About the Author. 99

INTRODUCTION

Mommy's Cooking Healthy is an inspirational work brought about by my transition to the *Vegan* lifestyle on September 12, 2017. After conducting my own personal research into how our bodies react to certain foods, I immediately knew I needed to change my eating habits and lifestyle for myself; but, more importantly, for my son Khyree. Don't get me wrong, I have always been conscious about eating mostly healthy and organic foods. However, I was surprised to learn that I wasn't as healthy as I thought I was.

Food is directly related to our health and plays a major role in our lives. It is very important that you pay close attention to what you allow into your Temple, as well as passing this knowledge down to your children. Certain foods and chemicals will definitely weaken their immune system, cause skin problems, and deteriorate brain cells. These issues could lead to an early death, comprehensive delays, and horrible behavior.

Once a child is born into this world, it is our responsibility as parents to control their eating habits. Although we all know that children and healthy foods rarely mix, there are many ways to provide them with more fruits and veggies to maintain a healthier lifestyle.

If you are an "On the Go" parent like me, I know that it is a challenge to work full-time and raise your children properly. Our lives are much easier with fast-food. Sometimes you are left with only that option because of how hectic your day was. This routine is easy, but it's extremely harmful to you and your children. You will need to decide what is more important. Your time? OR Their health?

Once you become accustomed to eating healthy, those fast-food meals will no longer be appealing to you or your children. Take the time to write down your daily goals and strategize your time frame. It certainly worked for me.

One

Becoming a Vegan (meat & dairy free) or a Vegetarian (meat free) has its pros and cons. Everyone's temple is different. As for my loved ones and I, we have personally witnessed benefits such as weight loss in adults, clearer skin, cancer cells minimized, and increased energy among those that have greatly reduced or eliminated meat, dairy, soy and gluten products.

Changing your eating habits could appear very challenging. Nevertheless, if you have the desire to live long enough to see your great great grandchildren, do not allow food to be the reason why your temple is suffering. Let's lead by example and together we will all have a greater chance of having the ability to enjoy our lives with our legacies. Let's Feed Our **Kids** Healthy Foods in a **K**osher, **I**ncredible, **D**elicious and **S**crumptious Way!

Love Always,

Alicia & Khyree

Good Morning My Sonshine

Kosher and Healthy Breakfast Dishes

Blueberry and Avocado Pancakes

Serves 2-4

Grocery List:

1 cup of wheat gluten free flour
½ cup of blueberries
2 tsp of avocado
1 ½ cup of Vanilla Almond Milk
2 tbsps. organic cinnamon sugar
2 tbsps. baking powder
Canola & Coconut Oil

Directions:

1. In a large bowl, blend the flour, baking powder and cinnamon sugar with a hand mixer. Add the blueberries, avocado and milk until the texture is smooth.
2. In a medium skillet, add the oil under medium high heat. Pour batter in the skillet to make the desired size pancakes. Flip the pancake after 5 minutes or once cradle begins to form around the rim of the pancake, it should be ready to flip. Cook the other side for 2 minutes. Spread non-dairy butter on top of each pancake.
3. Serve with organic maple syrup.

Sweet Potato Hash Bowl

Serves 2

Grocery List:

2 sweet potatoes (peeled & diced)

2 organic cage-free eggs

1 tbsp. of coconut milk

6 baby spinach leaves

1 yellow zucchini

¼ cup of diced green bell peppers

¼ cup of diced yellow bell peppers

¼ cup of diced orange bell peppers

Canola & Coconut oil

Salt & pepper for taste

Directions:

1. Place the diced sweet potatoes in a microwavable bowl for 3 minutes. (no water needed)
2. In a large non-stick skillet, add oil, sweet potatoes, zucchini and all of the peppers on medium heat for 20 minutes.
3. In a mixing bowl, scramble eggs and coconut milk with a spoon.
4. In a separate non-stick skillet, sauté the baby spinach for about 1 minute on medium heat. Add the egg mixture and cook eggs to desired texture.
5. Serve with the sweet potato hash in a bowl and place the egg with spinach on top.

Sausage & Spinach Breakfast Burrito

Serves 2

Grocery List:

2 Soft Vegan Flour Tortillas
4 Veggie Sausage Patties chopped
½ cup of non-dairy shredded
cheddar cheese

½ cup of spinach
Diced tomatoes
Diced onions
Olive oil

Directions:

1. In a medium sauce pan, sauté onions with olive oil. Stir in chopped veggie sausage patties until cooked thoroughly for 10 minutes. Add spinach and tomatoes.
2. Reduce the heat to simmer. Stir until spinach becomes limp. Turn off the heat. Sprinkle shredded cheese on top of the ingredients and allow the cheese to melt naturally.
3. In another nonstick or lightly greased pan, place tortilla in the pan and cook both sides for 3-5 minutes. Remove.
4. Placed ingredients on the far side and roll until the tortilla is in the burrito shape.
5. Serve.

Mini Breakfast Pizzas

Serves 4

Grocery List:

8 Soft Flour Tortillas

4 organic cage free eggs

2 tsp of coconut milk

4 Veggie Sausage Patties chopped

1 cup of non-dairy shredded cheddar cheese

1 cup of non-dairy shredded mozzarella cheese

3-5 baby spinach leaves

Diced green onions

Directions:

1. Preheat the oven at 350 degrees.
2. In a mixing bowl, whisk eggs and milk for 1 minute. In a cast iron skillet, add 1 tbsp of olive oil and spinach leaves on medium heat. Cook the egg mixture with the spinach leaves lightly. Place cooked eggs and spinach in a bowl to the side.
3. In a cast iron skillet, cook the chopped veggie sausage patties and onions with 1-2 tsp of olive oil until cooked thoroughly for 10 minutes. Turn off the heat.
4. On a nonstick baking sheet or lightly greased pan, place 2 tortillas on top of each other meaning you should have 4 pizzas to create. Spread a generous amount of cheese as your base, sausage mixture as the 2nd level then top off with more cheese.
5. Placed the pizzas in the oven for 20 minutes or until the cheese melts. Add the eggs and spinach mixture on top.
6. Serve.

Vegan Cinnamon Roll Bites

Serves 4-6

Grocery List:

Vegan Cinnamon Bites:

2 cups of gluten free whole wheat flour
1 cup of vanilla almond milk
2 tbsp of cinnamon sugar
2 tbsp of roasted cinnamon
1 cup of sugar
1/3 cup of brown sugar
2 tbsp of vegan butter (cold & cubed)
1 tbsp of vegan butter (melted)
1 tbsp of baking powder
½ tsp of salt

Vegan Cream Cheese Frosting

8 tbsp of vegan cream cheese
2 tbsp of vanilla almond milk
1 tsp of vanilla extract
1 stick of vegan butter (melted)
2 cups of sifter organic powdered sugar

Vegan Cinnamon Roll Bites

Directions:

1. Preheat oven at 350 degrees. Grease the sides and bottom with 1 tbsp melted butter.
2. In a mixing bowl, combine wheat flour, salt and baking powder. Add cubed butter with a fork until the butter is in small pieces. Stir in the almond milk slowly so that the dough as a blend.
3. In another mixing bowl, combine cinnamon sugar, roasted cinnamon, sugar and brown sugar until blended well.
4. On a floured counter top and flour on your hands, create ball shape bites and roll each bite into the cinnamon mixture. For more favorable bites blend the cinnamon mixture into the bites while rolling then in circular motions. Then place each bite onto the greased casserole dish. Top with 1 tbsp of melted butter. Sprinkle a little of the cinnamon mixture on top of the bites if you desire.
5. Bake for 30 minutes.

Vegan Cream Cheese Frosting

Directions:

1. In a large bowl, combine softened butter, vanilla extract, milk and vegan cream cheese until blended creamy and smooth.
2. Slowly add powdered sugar until the texture is blended at your desire.
3. Serve on top of the bites with lime zest.

Southern Grits and Bacon Bowl

Serves 4

Grocery List:

1 cup of coconut milk
4 cups of water
1 tbsp. of salt
1 cup of uncooked grits
3 tbsps. of butter
2 slices of cooked veggie bacon
½ cup of non-dairy shredded cheese

Directions:

1. In a large pot on medium high, combine water and salt until boiled. Add milk and reduce the heat.
2. Stir in grits with a wire whisk. Increase the heat to bowl then simmer for 25 minutes stirring occasionally.
3. Remove from heat. Add butter, bacon crumbs and cheese.
4. Serve in a bowl.

Apple Cinnamon Biscuits

Serves 4-6

Grocery List:

1 ½ cup of gluten free wheat flour

2 tsp of baking powder

½ tsp of salt

1 cup of cold coconut milk*

1 tsp of non-dairy butter

1 tbsp. of vanilla extract

1 tbsp. of almond milk

2 tbsps. of brown sugar

3 tsp of roasted cinnamon

3 peeled and sliced apples

1 tsp of applesauce (egg replacer)

½ cup of water

Directions:

1. Preheat oven at 450 degrees.
2. In a large mixing bowl, combine flour, baking powder and salt. Add applesauce then the cold milk slowly. Blend until the texture is smooth using your clean hands. Do NOT over blend the dough to avoid toughness. The texture should be tacky.
3. On a large cutting board, add flour to your hands and the cutting board. Create generous size biscuits using the flour and place on a greased baking sheet. Cook for 10-15 minutes or until biscuits are fluffy. Spread non-dairy butter on top and remove the biscuits out of the oven. Allow the butter to melt on its own.
4. Mix cinnamon, vanilla extract, brown sugar and milk in a medium bowl. In a greased casserole dish, layer the apple slices and spread the cinnamon mixture. Repeat until all apples are covered. Bake for 30 minutes, add water then bake for 10 more minutes or until the apples are tender.
5. Serve the biscuits with the cinnamon apple glaze on top.

Good Afternoon My Sonshine

Incredible and Healthy Lunch Dishes

Mini Corn Dog Muffin

Serves 3-6

Grocery List:

1 pkg of Veggie Hot Dogs (total of 8)
2 boxes of Vegetarian Corn Meal
2 egg replacers
1 can Coconut Milk

Directions:

1. Preheat oven at 350. In a large bowl, combine the cornmeal and coconut milk until blended well.
2. Cut the veggie hot dogs at desired bite size pieces. Stir the hot dogs in the cornmeal mixture.
3. In a non-stick or greased muffin pan, pour the batter into the muffin cup sections ¾ full.
4. Bake for 20 minutes or until the middle is done and golden yellow.
5. Serve with organic ketchup and mustard.

Fried Chicken

Serves 4- 6

Grocery List

Vegan Chicken Mixture:

1 cup of vital wheat gluten
4 tbsps. of nutritional yeast
1 tsp of onion powder
1 tsp garlic powder
1 tbsp. of cayenne pepper
1 tbsp. of creole seasonings
1 tbsp. of pepper
2 tbsps. of coconut milk
¾ cup of water
1 vegan chicken bouillon cube

Wet mixture:

¼ cup of coconut milk
¼ cup of water
2 tbsps. of stone ground mustard
½ tsp of garlic powder
½ tsp of pepper
1 cup of flour
1 tbsp. of nutritional yeast

Dry Mixture:

2 cups of flour
½ tsp of sea salt
1 tsp of pepper
4 tbsps. of nutritional yeast
1 tbsp. of cayenne pepper
2 tsp of baking powder
1 tbsp. of paprika

Directions:

1. In a mixing bowl, add all ingredients for the Vegan Chicken. Stir until blended well. Using your cleaned hands, spread and knead the dough for 30 seconds on a cutting board. Cut the dough in desired size pieces. The shape does not matter.

2. In a pot, place the vegan cube with 6 cups of water and bring to a boil. Then place the pieces of dough in the pot but reduce the heat to simmer for 30 minutes. Drain excess liquid with colander.

3. In another mixing bowl, mix all dry mixture ingredients with a spoon. In another mixing bowl, mix all the wet mixture ingredients with a wire whisk.

4. Dip each dough piece in the dry mixture then dip in the wet mixture then again in the dry mixture. After all pieces have been coated, fry the vegan chicken in desired temperature cooking skillet with olive oil until both sides are golden brown.

Twenty-nine

Mac n Cheese

Serves 2-4

Grocery List:

1 bag of dried elbow macaroni

1 bag of non-dairy shredded cheddar cheese

1 cup of cashew milk

½ pkg of non-dairy cream cheese (4 ounces)

1 stick of non-dairy butter (4 tbsps.)

¾ cup of bread crumbs

¼ cup of diced parsley

1 tsp of cayenne pepper

Salt and pepper for taste

Directions:

1. Preheat oven at 350. In a large pot, Boil the macaroni for 10 minutes with 1 tbsp of butter, drain and set to the side in a casserole dish.
2. In a pot, combine cashew milk, cream cheese and 2 tbsps. of butter on medium high heat. Once the ingredients have blended smoothly, add the cheese. Reduce heat and stir until the cheese melts.
3. Pour the cheese evenly on top of the macaroni. Add seasonings for taste and stir lightly for an even blend.
4. In a small saucepan on medium heat, combine 1 tbsp of butter along with freshly chopped parsley until the butter melts. Pour the butter and parsley evenly on top of the macaroni. Sprinkle bread crumbs.
5. Bake uncover for 15-20 minutes or until golden brown.
6. Serve.

Cheese Dip

Serves 6-8

Grocery List:

1 bag of meatless grounds
2 bags of non-dairy shredded cheddar cheese
1 can of black beans (drained and cleaned)
1 cup of coconut milk
1 Tomato (diced)
1 onion (diced)
½ cup of green onions (diced)
1 tsp of jalapeño

Directions:

1. In a non-stick skillet on medium heat, brown the meatless grounds and onions for 15 minutes. Season for taste
2. In a cast iron pot on medium heat, combine milk and cheese. Stir until cheese melts then reduce the heat.
3. Pour meatless grounds into the pot with the cheese mixture. Add black beans, tomatoes, green onions and jalapenos. Stir and let simmer for 10 minutes.
4. Serve with gluten free tortilla chips.

Fiesta Black Bean Fries

Serves 4-6

Grocery List:

1 bag of fries
2 cans of Black Beans
1 cup of diced tomatoes & green chilies
½ cup of diced green onions
Salt & pepper for taste
Ketchup

Directions:

1. Pre-heat oven at 350 degrees. On a baking sheet, use an olive oil spray to coat the bottom of the sheet. In a large bowl, pour the frozen fries and season well with Cajun season salt. Place the fries on the sheet and spread them in a single layer.
2. Bake for 15 minutes and sprinkle the diced green onions on top of the fries. Bake for another 15-20 minutes or until fries are golden brown and crisp.
3. While the fries are cooking, mix the black beans, tomatoes and chiles in a cast iron pot on medium heat. Stir for 10 minutes.
4. In a bowl, place fries and pour the fiesta beans on top covered with ketchup.
5. Serve.

GRILLED CHEESE SANDWICHES WITH TOMATO SOUP

Serves 4-6

Grocery List:

Sliced non-dairy cheddar cheese
Vegan Sliced Bread
4 Tbsp unsalted non-dairy butter
1 onion (diced)
1 cup of freshly pureed tomatoes
2 cups of organic vegetable broth (make sure the ingredients are dairy, meat & soy free)
Sea Salt for taste

Directions:

1. In a cast iron pot, melt butter on medium heat. Add the onions, broth, tomatoes and salt. Reduce heat to simmer. Stir occasionally for 30 minutes until soup is blended well.
2. In a large non-stick skillet, place two slices of buttered bread in the pan. Add one slice of cheese on each bread. Once the cheese begins to melt, use a spatula to make the sandwich where the cheese sides are together. Cut sandwich in half diagonally.
3. Serve soup with sandwich on the side.

Black Bean Burgers

Serves 2

Grocery List:

1 can of black beans (well drained)
1 cup of bread crumbs
½ chopped yellow onions
1 tsp of garlic powder
1 tsp of onion powder
flour
Smoked sea salt and pepper for taste

Directions:

1. Preheat oven on 350 F.
2. In a large bowl, mash the black beans until smooth like paste. In a cast iron skillet, sauté onions for 5 minutes. Add the sautéed onions, black beans bread crumbs garlic powder and onion powder into a mixture.
3. Add a generous amount of flour to the mixture a few tablespoons at a time. Form the black bean mixture into patties of your desired size (preferably ½ thick).
4. Place burgers on a non-stick pan (preferably a cast iron pan). Sprinkle a dash of salt and pepper for taste. Bake for 15-20 minutes.
5. Serve on fresh baked buns, fully dressed. Seasoned potato wedges and ketchup as a side dish.

GOOD EVENING MY SONSHINE

Delicious and Healthy Dinner Dishes

Meatless Chicken Salad

Serves 6

Grocery List:

1 bag of meatless chicken

1/2 cup of Vegan Mayo

3 tbsp of Organic Mustard

2 tsp of sweet relish

1 tsp of Diced Jalapeño Peppers

1 cup of diced green onions

1 tsp of cayenne pepper

1 tsp of sea salt and pepper

1 tbsp of season salt

Canola & coconut oil

Directions:

1. Heat 2-3 teaspoons of oil in a large skillet over medium heat. Add the meatless chicken in a skillet over medium heat for 10-12 minutes. Add desired seasonings thoroughly while stirring.
2. Let the meatless chicken cool for about 5 minutes in a large bowl. Chopped the meatless chicken into shreds of desired pieces on a cutting board. Place the pieces back in the bowl.
3. Mix the meatless chicken, vegan mayo and mustard until the texture is at your desire taste. Stir peppers, relish and diced green onions until the ingredients form a smooth texture. Top off with a pinch of cayenne pepper for taste and garnishment.
4. Serve with flatbread crackers or fresh oven baked buns as sandwiches.

CHILI BEANS WITH CORNBREAD

Serves 6

Grocery List:

1 bag of meatless grounds
1 can of Pinto Beans
1 can of Black Beans
1 can of Kidney Beans
1 can of tomato sauce (16 oz)
1 package of Vegetarian Chili Mix
½ cup of diced Jalapeños

½ cup of diced onions
½ cup of diced green onions
1 cup of diced organic tomatoes
½ cup of diced parsley
Season salt, salt & pepper for taste
¼ of warm water

Directions:

1. In a large cast iron pot, brown the meatless grounds for 10-15 minutes along with the Jalapenos, onions, green onions and season salt. Drain as much of the excess liquid with a colander.
2. To the pot, add water, tomatoes, parsley, beans, chili mix and water. Stir until all ingredients create a perfect blend. Then add the tomato sauce along with the meatless meat. Add sea salt, pepper for taste per your desire.
3. Simmer for about 20 minutes.
4. Serve over Cauliflower Rice or organic rice.

Cornbread

Grocery List:

1 box of gluten-free cornmeal mix
1 can Coconut Milk (12 oz.)
1 egg replacer
¼ of diced Jalapeños
Olive oil
Non-dairy butter

Directions:

1. Preheat oven on 350 F to 375 F.
2. Grease 8-inch pan with a dash of olive oil. Place in oven for 5 minutes.
3. Mix all ingredients in a large boil until texture is smooth. Remove pan out of oven and pour the batter into the pan.
4. Place in oven for 20-25 minutes. Once cooked thoroughly, spread non-dairy butter and allow the butter to melt from the hot cornbread.
5. Serve with the Chili Beans.

Lasagna

Serves 6

Grocery List:

1 bag of meatless grounds
1 Jar of Tomato
Sauce Mixture
1 can of Tomato
Paste (16 oz.)
1 can of organic
crushed tomatoes

2 Tbsp of fresh
basil (chopped)
1 whole onion (diced)
1 bay leaf
1 tbsp. of fresh
grounded garlic
¼ cup of parsley

1 pkg of organic lasagna
noodles (12 oz)
3-5 cups of shredded non-
dairy mozzarella cheese
Smoked Sea Salt, Pepper &
Italian seasonings for taste

Directions:

1. Preheat the oven to 375 F. Spray a 9x13- inch baking dish with olive oil cooking spray.
2. In a large cast iron pot, sauté the diced onions with a little of olive oil along with seasoning with the garlic, smoked sea salt and pepper. Add the meatless grounds, Italian seasonings and bay leaf for 10-15 minutes. Drain excess liquids with a colander.
3. Add tomato sauce, the jar of tomato mixture sauce, crushed tomatoes and fresh basil. Simmer for 20 minutes. Turn off the heat and remove the Bay Leaf.
4. Boil the lasagna noodles for 10 minutes with olive oil and parsley. Drain excess water with a colander.
5. Layer bottom of the baking dish with meatless sauce (1/2 cup is recommended). Top with one layer of lasagna noodles. Sprinkle with cheese. Add meatless sauce then more cheese. Repeat this pattern by ending with the rest of the cheese of your desire.
6. Using the olive oil baking spray, coat desired sheet of aluminum foil and cover baking dish. This way the cheese will not stick to the foil. Bake for 60 minutes. Uncover, sprinkle more cheese and bake for an additional 10-15 minutes until the noodles are tender.

Jambalaya

Serves 6

Grocery List:

1 bag of Meatless Sausage

1 bag of Meatless Chicken

2 cups of rice

2 bell peppers (diced)

1 whole onion (diced)

2 stalks of celery (diced)

1 can of diced tomatoes (12 oz)

1 tbsp of Paprika

½ cup of Creole Seasonings

1 tbsp of Garlic (grounded)

4-5 cups of Vegetable Broth (double check the ingredients to avoid meat products)

2 tbsp of Organic Cumin

1 tsp of dried thyme

1 tsp of dried oregano

1 tbsp of olive oil

1 tsp of Vegan Worcestershire sauce

Directions:

1. In a large cast iron pot, sauté the sliced meatless sausage and the meatless chicken with olive oil for 10-15 minutes or until the meatless meat is fully cooked. Add the diced onion, garlic, green bell peppers and celery. Stir for 5 minutes.
2. Stir in the rice, tomatoes and creole seasonings. Add vegetable broth, Worcestershire sauce, diced oregano, thyme and cumin. Bring to a boil for 10 minutes then reduce heat to medium-low. Add paprika for taste. Simmer until rice is ready.
3. Serve with vegan cornbread and cabbage.

Taco Pizza

Serves 4-6

Grocery List:

1 box of cauliflower pizza crust

1 bag of meatless meat

1 pack of Gluten free Taco Seasonings

1 bag of non-dairy shredded Cheddar Cheese

1 bag of finely shredded green leaf lettuce

½ cup of purple onions

½ cup of jalapenos

2 tomatoes diced

Mild or Hot Taco Sauce

1/3 cup of water

Directions:

1. Preheat oven on 350 F.
2. In a cast iron skillet, brown the meatless meat with olive oil and onions for 10-15 minutes. Drain excess liquids with a colander. Add water and taco seasonings. Cook for 5 minutes.
3. Place pizza crust on a non-stick pizza pan. Sprinkled desired amount of non-dairy cheese onto the crust. Add the meatless grounds, more onions and jalapenos. Sprinkle more cheese.
4. Bake pizza for 20 minutes or until crust is cooked and cheese has melted. Remove from oven.
5. Add diced tomatoes and shredded lettuce. Finish with desired coat of taco sauce.
6. Serve.

Meatless Meatloaf with Broccoli, Cheese & Cauliflower Rice

Serves 6

Grocery List:

Meatless Meatloaf:

4 Plant-Based Burger Patties (thawed)
1 pack of McCormick Meat Loaf seasoning mix
2 egg replacers (prepared) *
½ cup of cashew milk
¼ cup of bread crumbs

Rice:

2 bags of steamed cauliflower rice
2 tbsp of non-dairy butter
6 cups of chopped broccoli (cooked)
½ cup of diced onions
2 tbsp of flour
2 cups of cashew milk
1 tsp of garlic powder
1 tsp of salt and pepper
½ tsp of paprika
½ tsp of dry ground mustard seeds
2 tsp of cream cheese
1 block of vegan cheddar cheese

Directions:

1. Pre-heat the oven at 350 degrees.
2. In a large bowl, combine the patties, seasoning mix, egg replacers and bread crumbs until well blended. Add milk and stir until the ingredients are mixed into the patties evenly. Form the loaf into a meatloaf pan. Bake for 1 hour.
3. In a cast iron pot on medium heat, combine butter and onions. Once the butter has melted, add flour, garlic, paprika, ground mustard seeds and cream cheese. Stir in the cashew milk slowly with a wire whisk. Once the mixture comes to a boil, remove from heat and add the cheese. Keep stirring until the cheese melts. (may need to place back on simmer heat if cheese does not melt fast enough) Add the broccoli.
4. In a greased casserole dish, add rice and mixture. Stir until evenly blended. Bake for 35 minutes.
5. Serve best with brown gravy on loaf and rice as the side.

*If you do not like Cauliflower rice, you may replace
it with 2 cups of cooked organic rice.

Vegetarian Red Beans

Serves 6-8

Grocery List:

1 lb of pre-soaked drained kidney beans (be sure to soak beans in water and kosher salt for at least 24 hours or soak in boiling water for an hour)
1 tbsp of olive oil
1 lb of finely cooked chopped meatless sausage
1 large onion (diced)
1 green pepper (diced)

3 stalks of finely chopped celery
2 cloves of minced garlic
1 tbsp of cayenne pepper
Salt and pepper for taste
Liquid smoke
2 tbsp of thyme
2 bay leaves

Directions:

1. In a large cast iron pot, add olive oil, cooked meatless sausage, onions, celery and bell peppers. Season with creole seasonings per your desire and stir for 10 minutes. Add garlic and liquid smoke. Stir for a minute. Add cayenne pepper and grounded pepper. Continue stirring for a minute. Add the beans with water, thyme and bay leaves.
2. Bring to a boil for 20 minutes then reduce heat to simmer. Cover and allow beans to cook for 2 hours or until the beans are at desired texture.
3. Once the liquid has thickened beyond desired taste, add more water. Repeat until desired appearance is upon your satisfaction.
4. Serve red beans over rice.

SEVEN SNACKS

Scrumptious and Healthy Snacks

Honey BBQ Cauliflower Bites

Grocery List:

1 head of fresh cauliflower

1 cup of gluten free flour

½ cup of coconut milk

½ cup of water

Season salt for taste

1 tbsp of honey mustard

2 tbsp of brown sugar

1 tsp of honey

1 bottle of Vegan BBQ sauce

Directions:

1. Preheat the oven at 350 degrees.
2. Wash the head of cauliflower and break the pieces in the desired size pieces to emulate boneless drumettes/wings. Season the bites lightly with desired amount of season salt. Set the pieces in a bowl.
3. In a large bowl, combine the flour and milk with a whisk. Add 1-3 tbsp of water until the batter is smooth.
4. While dipping each piece of cauliflower into the batter, place the pieces on a non-stick baking sheet. Bake for 30 minutes.
5. While the cauliflower is baking, combine honey mustard, brown sugar, honey, 1 tbsp of water and BBQ sauce in a saucepan. Stir for 10 minutes and let simmer for 5 minutes.
6. Take cauliflower out of the oven. Using a fork, dip each piece into the BBQ sauce and place back on the baking sheet. Bake for 15 minutes.
7. Serve with celery sticks and vegan ranch.

Kiddie Trail Mix

Grocery List:

1 cup of Whole Grain Cereal

1 cup of raisins

1 cup of mini pretzels (twist or sticks)

1 cup of plain chocolate candy

½ cup of peanuts (optional if child is not allergic)

Directions:

1. Mix all of the ingredients in a large container and store in a cool place.
2. Serve as an afternoon snack.

Fruit Bowls with Non-Dairy Cream Cheese Avocado Dip

Grocery List:

8 oz of Non-Dairy Cream Cheese
½ cup of light brown sugar
1 tbsp of vanilla extract
2 tbsp of avocado
1 tsp of almond milk
4 different types of desired fruit

Directions:

1. Using a hand mixer, beat the cream cheese until the texture is whipped. Add the vanilla extract, brown sugar and avocado. Add the almond milk and continue to blend until the texture is smooth.
2. Cut the fruit at the desired sizes that are suitable for your child.
3. Serve.

Celery Sticks with Peanut Butter

Grocery List:

Celery Sticks (pre-cut and cleaned)
1 cup of non-dairy yogurt
3 tbsp of organic honey
4 tbsp of creamy organic peanut butter

Directions:

1. In a bowl, mix yogurt, peanut butter and honey.
2. Serve with celery.

Apple & Almond Butter Toast

Grocery List:

1 cup of almonds
1 red organic apple (sliced and cleaned)
Wheat toast

Directions:

1. Pre-heat oven on 350 degrees.
2. On a non-stick pan, spread the almonds and bake for 10-15 minutes.
3. Using a food processor, place the almonds and allow the food processor to transform the almonds into a creamy texture. Stir when needed. Keep in mind that once you notice the almonds form into a ball, the process is almost done.
4. Spread the almond butter on the toast. Place 3-4 slices of apple on the toast.
5. Serve.

Strawberry Kiwi Kale Popsicles

Grocery List:

4 oz of Coconut water
4 oz of Apple Juice
1 ½ cup of fresh strawberries
1 cup of fresh peeled kiwis
1 cup of finely chopped kale

Directions:

1. In a blender, combine coconut water, apple juice, strawberries, kiwis and kale. Keep a few strawberries and kiwis to the side.
2. Once the mixture is completely blended, place at least 1 strawberry and 1 kiwi in the popsicle holder. Fill up the holder with the mixture.
3. Freeze overnight.
4. Serve the next day as an afternoon snack.

Fruit Smoothie

Grocery List:

1 cup of almond milk
1 cup of non-dairy yogurt of your choice
½ cup of frozen strawberries
2 tbsp of avocado
1 tsp of ground flaxseed

Directions:

1. Place all ingredients in a blender for 3-5 minutes.
2. Serve in your child's favorite cup.

Welcome to Hydration Station

Below are some fruit and vegetable water infusions that are kid-friendly.
These drinks keep our kids hydrated in a fun and healthy way!

Watermelon, Cucumber, Kiwi and Mint

- Watermelons contain 91% water and 7.5% of carbs. It contains no protein or fat.
- Cucumbers contain 95.2% water. They support the heart and fights inflammation as well as reduce risk of cancer
- Kiwi improves your skin, eyes and heart health. Contains vitamin E and is a high antioxidant fruit.
- Mint contains potassium, magnesium, calcium, phosphorus, vitamin C, iron and vitamin A.

Strawberry, Cucumber, Lime and Mint

- Limes reduce the risk of asthma and promote healthy skin. One lime can provide 32% of the vitamin C needed a day.

Orange, Cucumber, Lemon and Mint

- Oranges are a great source of fiber and Vitamin C.

Strawberry, Blueberry, Lemon and Mint

- Strawberries contain 91% of water. Contains folate (B9), potassium, vitamin C and manganese.
- Blueberries boost brain health, support digestion and high in antioxidants.
- Lemons contain 89% of water. Contains Vitamin B6, potassium and vitamin C. They improve your moods and decrease stress.

Encouraging and Inspirational Words from Loved Ones

In the same way, let your light shine before others, so that they may see your good works and give glory to your Father who is in heaven.

Matthew 5:16 NKJV

1. This book is absolutely amazing. I truly thank God for Blessing you with the vision to see how much of an inspiration you are to so many people. I've personally been contemplating about my food choices for a long time. I knew that I needed to eat healthier, but I was skeptical about leaving my favorite foods alone. Never would have guessed in a million years that I could enjoy life by eating plants. Thanks to you, I was introduced to the plant-

based lifestyle and quickly discovered that I can still eat my favorite foods while greatly improving my health. From hamburgers and chicken salad, to lasagna and chili beans... I was amazed to eat the various meals you have prepared for me, especially knowing they are all plant based and absolutely delicious. I am so very grateful for you and thank you for changing my life. I am sure that this book will benefit many people as it is practical and priceless!

Stephen Tweedle
Baton Rouge, LA
#WGT4

2. Every recipe my daughter created tasted so good. She served it with a smile and I was content eating it because I knew she was cooking with the concern about the human body. She desired all of us to stop eating meat, so she cooked our favorite meals in a healthy way. Then one morning while I was praying, Jesus said, "Tell her to do a cookbook." Once I shared my spiritual conversation with my daughter, she lit up, smiled and revealed the confirmation of His Words to her. I have watched her cook every recipe with so much joy. I now have confirmation this is her voice and she speak well.

Carla Patrice Spurlock
Baton Rouge, LA

3. The Vegan dishes are new to me but I was delighted to taste the BBQ cauliflower bites and fiesta black bean fries. I will be trying these two meals again because eating healthy is not that bad at all. Alicia makes the meals taste so good that you are forgetting that you are eating healthy. As Khyree's father, Khyree inspires me to think about eating healthier because I know that his mother will never stop feeding him the right way. I am truly proud of them both.

Marcus Jackson
Baker, LA

4. This Meatless Chicken Salad was WONDERFUL. I remember saying, "chicken has to be in this because of the texture". After being convinced that it was meatless, I decided I would love the recipe and prepare it myself. Congratulations on your book!

Ms. Katherine Tweedle
Detroit, MI

5. We love a vegan lifestyle but being a truck driver it's hard to maintain that lifestyle on the road. A vegan diet really gives us more energy and really helps with fatigue. One of the best meals we had was a spaghetti dish by Alicia Johnson. She used Quorn meat crumbles, which were a great substitute. Her sauce was her own recipe using a tomato base, other vegetables and spices. Her sauce was bursting with flavor. Not sure of the brand of spaghetti she used, but it had a great texture to it. The meal overall was put together very well, full of flavor, and very enjoyable.

Kevin & Janice Johnson
Dallas, TX

6. The Meatless Chicken Salad taste really good. My brother requested this meal for a small family reunion. I was a little skeptical at first, but it was well seasoned and extra delicious with bread. I would've never known it didn't have meat in it, if I wasn't told. Alicia really knows how to turn health foods into soul foods.

Erika James
Jonesboro, AR

7. You have impacted my life by always encouraging me to eat clean. You have educated me on the different meat substitutes or plant-based foods that are offered in stores. I must say that I was kind of skeptical at first, but your recommendations were DELICIOUS! Your constant commitment to eating what's best for the body is inspiring to me. All I know is that if you eat it then so can I. I trust you!

Jamal Cain
Baton Rouge, LA

8. My cousin Alicia is always the one to try something different with her body. She is not a dieter, but she always watches what she eats and how her body adapts to it. She is the one who will figure out any remedies for an illness and I call her my Health coach. When she became a vegan, she took it seriously. I am contemplating on becoming a vegan myself, but I know that I am absolutely proud of her!

Dedrick Harbor
Baton Rouge, LA

9. I honestly can't find the words to express how happy and proud of you I am. We've been through so much together during our friendship and to see you follow your dreams and turn your love and dedication to leading a healthy lifestyle, not only for you but for your son and others around you is truly amazing. I know all the hard work, tears, faith and passion you've poured into this book will not be in vain. You are truly a remarkable woman and an astounding mother. I am so blessed to have you as my best friend and I wish you all the success, happiness, and blessings your heart desires. Always keep moving forward and continue to strive for greatness.

LaToya Thomas
Denham Springs, LA

10. Every dish that my sister cooks is just fantastic especially the meatless meatloaf. I love her food so much!

Akeem Johnson
Baton Rouge, LA

11. As Khyree's grandmother, I am so proud that he is eating healthy foods starting at a young age. I must say that the non-meat chicken salad is the best thing I have ever tasted.

Joyce Jackson
Baker, LA

12. The journey to here wasn't easy and the continuation will not always be easy but your Faith, devotion, courage and grit has brought you a long way. The change in your eating habits has not only impacted your life but you have influenced your family, friends and even strangers. You are blazing a trail for women all over and laying a foundation and building a legacy for your son. May you continue to be Blessed in your future endeavors. I am very very PROUD of you. I am overjoyed to see where this journey will lead you. You "BETA" believe it! (insider)

Donta Mills
Ponchatoula, LA

13. You have inspired me in so many ways. You have overcome obstacles in your life and you are still smiling. You have shown me how God is working with you and through you. I am very proud of the woman you have become. I love you so much!!!!!!

Sharita Heckard
Houston, TX

TESTIMONIAL REVIEWS

My First Vegan/Vegetarian Tasting was held in Baton Rouge, LA 8/17/2018. I prepared 3 dishes for my co-workers to sample which were Meatless Chicken Salad served with a Flatbread cracker, Vegetarian Cheese Dip served with gluten-free tortillas and Vegetarian Chili Beans served alone. Below are honest opinions from those who are either meat lovers or not fans of vegetables:

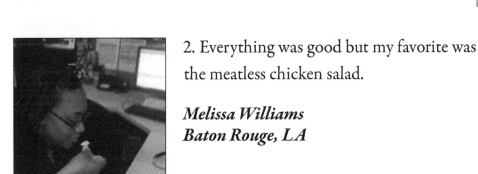

1. I loved EVERYTHING but the Chili Beans were absolutely fantastic. I could not tell the meatless chicken salad was not made with real chicken. So Delicious!

   Deborah Robinson
   Baton Rouge, LA

2. Everything was good but my favorite was the meatless chicken salad.

   Melissa Williams
   Baton Rouge, LA

3. The Chili was EXCELLENT. I would not have known it was vegan if I wasn't told. The flavor and texture were outstanding.

Jason Rabalais
Baton Rouge, LA

4. The meatless chicken salad was AWESOME. This is making me want to go Vegan.

Michelle Grimes
Baker, LA

5. Courtney Barrett (right) from Denham Springs, LA stated this: "I tasted the meatless chicken salad and chili and they were both Great." Tiffani Williams (left) from Baton Rouge, LA stated this: "Absolutely delicious! The chili was so full of flavor and perfect texture."

6. The chili beans were awesome!

Brandy Hutton
Walker, LA

7. I absolutely loved the cheese dip and chili. I am so excited about Alicia's Cookbook!

Charmecia Gallow
Baton Rouge, LA

8. The food is very good and tasteful.

   Michelle Chacon
   Zachary, LA

9. The meatless chicken salad was the BEST! The taste was everything to say it's a vegan dish. I loved, loved, LOVED IT! Thanks Alicia

   Carlisha Curtis
   Baton Rouge, LA

10. The food was honestly incredible. I have considered eating in a healthier way for a while but always thought healthy food was not as good. But this experience has certainly changed my opinion. It was so delicious.

    Emily Montgomery
    Baton Rouge, LA

11. Loved, Loved IT!! I didn't know healthy food could taste so good!

    Vicki Futrell
    Holden, LA

12. I especially loved the chili beans. However, both dishes were delicious. I really don't like beans in my chili but sometimes I tolerate the beans and I like the taste of her chili beans.

    Karlonda Abercrombie
    Baton Rouge, LA

13. Bernadine Lorraine (left) from Baton Rouge, LA stated: "I truly enjoyed everything. It was almost as if you could taste the time, dedication and love put into every bite. Great Job Alicia! I pray much success to you." April Waites (right) from Baker, LA stated: "The Meatless Chicken Salad hands down was the best chicken salad I have ever tasted. It was truly DA BOMB! I LOVE me some Chili and this Vegetarian Chili was very good. I could not tell that it was made with meatless grounds. As far as the flavor, there was nothing missing. This Chili will be great during the winter months to keep you warm and healthy. The Vegetarian Cheese Dip was awesome! I love cheese and this dip was great. It will be a great addition to any party as an appetizer or just as an anytime snack."

14. The Meatless Chicken Salad was good, but the Vegetarian Cheese Dip was delicious. LOVE, LOVE, LOVE IT!!!!!

Youlanda Hunter
Denham Springs, LA

15. Tammy Cuvillier (right) from Gonzales, LA stated: "The chili was my favorite. I could not tell it was not ground meat. The flavor and seasonings were fantastic. The chicken salad had a great flavor as well. The cheese dip was good but was not as "cheesy" as I expected but none the less still very good." Maegan Delaune (left) from Gonzales, LA stated: "I am an extreme meat lover and was very skeptical, but this was DELICIOUS!!! Would love your meatless chicken salad and chili recipe.

ACKNOWLEDGEMENTS

When you have Faith and put the work behind it, it gives God the opportunity to move on your behalf. Without God's Grace and Mercy, I would be nothing at all. For He provided me with every thought, every person and every source in order to accomplish this beautiful goal. I thank God for His guidance, His Love and His Protection.

To my son, mommy LOVES YOU TO THE MOON AND BACK! We did it! We have published our first of many cookbooks to come. Mommy thanks you and your dad, Marcus Jackson for trusting me with your life. I will do everything in my power to protect you. I will always try to protect you from harmful foods and harmful people. Always remember to eat your vitamins, vegetables and fruits. And once you learn how to read, read your labels. I love you Khyree D'Marcus Jackson.

Momma, I have witnessed you give to me more than you have given yourself. Your sacrifices since the day I was born will never go unnoticed. Although we struggled as kids, you slowly introduced us to healthier foods day by day. You are the first person I have ever seen eat organic foods. I can honestly say that you gave me my first insight of eating right. Your daily inspirational words have kept me focused on becoming a better version of myself. While bringing my recipes to life, you held my head up during my most discouraging moments. I thank you for believing in me and being my visible angel. I love you Carla Patrice Spurlock.

Daddy, our relationship has been stronger than ever. God's timing is the perfect timing. Your heart is so genuine that does not require recognition. Meaning, you do things without asking for credit. That is the kind of love that everyone should have. I thank you for guiding me in the right direction with not eating meat or dairy products from your countless list of documentaries. You and Mrs. Janice have grown to find the fundamental facts of how our lives could change if we did the proper research. I thank you both for investing in me and loving me. I love you Kevin Roy Johnson, Sr.

Stephen, our friendship has grown into something so special. No matter how much you have going on, how fatigued you may appear, you are always helping me. I had many nights of venting and crying because of my overthinking and struggling moments. I can honestly say that your Faith in God gives me the strength to keep pushing and to become a better Christian. When the odds are against me, you support me. Thank you for helping me create a series of foods that I am proud of. I believe that you have read my book more than I have. That is a true friend that holds true love. Your loyalty will never go unnoticed and I thank God for our paths being crossed. I love you Stephen Tweedle. #WGT4

Alieyah Johnson, thank you sis for being my set designer and photographer. We did it baby girl! The sweat, blood and tears were worth it. Your beautiful spirit and comical personality kept my energy positive while cooking each meal with soul. It is very important that I thank my baby brother, Akeem Johnson, for being my food taster. I will never forget your honest criticism and compliments. I needed every word you spoke, because your honesty allowed me to adjust my recipes when necessary. Thank you sis, Patrice Johnson for allowing my photo shoot to be held at your beautiful home. Thank you sis, Ashley Johnson for sampling my foods along with my nephews. My brother, Kevin Johnson, I love you. I cannot wait to have you as a guest on one of my cooking shows in the future.

For my work family, you are some awesome human beings. Thank you for being the first group of individuals to participate at one of many Vegan/Vegetarian Tastings to come.

I am so humbled that I have people in my life that truly support my every move. It is amazing how small my circle is yet the love I have retained while completing my first cookbook was phenomenally received from a lot of people. The appreciation that I have in my heart is indescribable. As the tears fell from my eyes the moment I received my first completed cookbook, all I could do is thank God and the people that helped my dream become a reality.

INDEX

Applesauce

Bananas

Basil

Bay leaves

BBQ sauce

Bell peppers

Black beans

Bouillon cube

Bread crumbs

Brown sugar

Butter

Cajun season salt

Canned tomatoes

Cashew milk

Cauliflower

Cauliflower pizza crust

Cayenne pepper

Celery

Cheddar Cheese

Chiles

Cinnamon sugar

Coconut milk

Corn meal

Cream cheese

Crushed tomatoes

Cumin

Dried elbow macaroni

Eggs

Flour tortillas

Fries

Frozen strawberries

Garlic

Garlic powder

Gluten free flour

Green onions

Grits

Ground flaxseed

Honey

Honey mustard

Instant yeast

Jalapenos

Kidney beans

Lasagna noodles

Lettuce

Liquid smoke

Mayo

Meatless chicken

Meatless grounds

Meatless sausage

Mild taco sauce

Mozzarella cheese

Non-dairy yogurt

Nutritional yeast

Olive oil

Onion powder

Oregano

Paprika

Parsley

Pickles

Pinto beans

Powdered sugar

Rice

Rolled oats

Salt

Spinach

Stone ground mustard

Sugar

Taco seasonings

Thyme

Tomato paste

Tomato sauce

Tomatoes

Vanilla almond milk

Vegetable broth

Vegetarian chili mix

Veggie bacon

Veggie hot dogs

Veggie sausage patties

Vital Wheat gluten

Wheat flour

Whole wheat bread

Worcestershire sauce

ABOUT THE AUTHOR

On October 19, 1984, Alicia Alexandria Johnson was born in New Iberia, LA. As the eldest of 5 siblings, she was raised in Baton Rouge, LA with spiritual love. She was taught how to value the importance of Family, Faith and Compassion.

Alicia's adolescent years were a struggle due to her personal insecurities. She endured the stress of childhood obesity, bullies and low self-esteem. However, Alicia never gave up on herself.

Studied Mathematics at Southeastern Louisiana University in Hammond, LA, she began to discover the beauty contained within her smile and her spirit of compassion towards others. She developed a genuine love for encouraging and inspiring others.

She began to pay more attention to her personal health. Better food choices and daily exercise became priorities in her life. Her self-esteem was restored quickly.

On July 20, 2015, Alicia gave birth to her son Khyree. Her number one priority was to ensure that he would be healthy for positive growth and development.

After some trial and error with conventional Pediatricians, Alicia was not satisfied with the recommendations given in order to maintain a healthy lifestyle for her son. Her extensive research led to the realization that one of the most common sources of illnesses or disorders, is the chemicals in foods.

Alicia has not only improved the life of herself and her son, but she has been an inspiration to countless others that can all attest to the amazing benefits Alicia has to offer humanity.

Alicia is in the development phase of programs which will contribute to the overall health and wellness of local schools and the communities in which they serve. As she has found her passion and purpose in life by improving her own health, she is dedicated to helping as many others as possible to do the same.